CRISPIN
THE CROSS OF LEAD

by
Avi

Teacher Guide

Written by
Judith L. Martin

Edited by
Monica Odle

Note

The first edition, hardcover version of this book, published by Hyperion Books, ©2002, was used to prepare this guide. Page references may vary in other editions.

Please note: Parts of this novel deal with sensitive, mature issues. Please assess the appropriateness of this book for the age level and maturity of your students prior to reading and discussing it with them.

ISBN 1-58130-804-3

To order, contact your local school supply store, or—
Novel Units, Inc.
P.O. Box 97
Bulverde, TX 78163-0097

Web site: www.educyberstor.com

Table of Contents

Skills and Strategies

Thinking
Identifying attributes, compare/contrast, synthesizing, research, evaluating

Vocabulary
Context clues, suffixes, multiple meanings, parts of speech, synonyms, antonyms, antiquated words, oxymororns

Listening/Speaking
Dramatization, discussion, speaking, monologue

Comprehension
Predicting, summarizing, cause and effect, inference, main idea, analyzing

Writing
Descriptive, narrative, compare/contrast, explanation, dialogue/play

Literary Elements
Characterization, setting, plot development, irony, theme development, foreshadowing, humor, figurative language

Across the Curriculum
Social Studies—maps, Middle Ages, culture; Math—measurement, money; Music—instruments, songs; Technology—graphics, word processing, PowerPoint presentation, desktop publishing

Genre: historical fiction

Setting: England, Middle Ages, 1377

Point of View: first-person

Themes: identity, freedom, self-reliance, survival

Conflict: person vs. person, person vs. self

Tone: suspense and optimism

Date of First Publication: 2002

Summary

Asta's son/Crispin, a 13-year-old orphan, narrates the story of his adventures. Wrongly accused of theft and murder, he flees his small village of Stromford and meets a jester named Bear. They travel to Great Wexly, where Bear brings news to a secret underground political group and tries to protect Crispin from the people who want to kill him. Crispin discovers his own identity and gains confidence and freedom.

Teacher Notes

The novel is based in 1377, and while most of the characters are fictitious, the conditions and events described are historically based. John Ball, a character in the story, was a real person of the time who fought against the poor treatment of serfs. The book focuses on the hardships of the peasants (90% of the population) and the tyranny of the nobles and their assistants. The class may benefit by focusing on both of the following themes—the hardships of rural and village life, and the romanticized "knignts and castles" theme.

The novel, accurate to the time period, highlights the strong role the Christian church played in the everyday life of the feudal system. Some teachers may choose to notify parents that there are numerous references to God, saints, the devil, the church, prayer, and canonical laws. The class may discuss these as historical elements. The Crusades are briefly mentioned in the novel, but they took place almost 200 years before the novel's setting.

About the Author

Avi (Ah-vee) Wortis was born in 1937 in New York City to his father, a psychiatrist, and his mother, a social worker. He liked to doodle and draw as a child in Brooklyn. His extended family includes a painter, a composer, and other writers. Avi credits his family's love of reading as the foundation for his writing ability. His family members were also involved with social activism to work against racism and for women's rights and labor.

Avi's difficulties in school, due to what was later diagnosed as dysgraphia, did not discourage him from writing. A tutor taught him the basics in writing the summer before his senior year in high school and encouraged his creativity. He attended Antioch University and later the University of Wisconsin in Madison, avoiding English classes and enrolling in playwriting classes. One of his plays won an award and was published in a magazine. He worked a variety of jobs before securing a position in the theater collection of the New York Public Library. He earned his master's degree at night from Columbia University in library science and worked as a librarian for 25 years.

A friend who was writing a children's book asked Avi to illustrate it. The publisher, impressed with his drawings, asked Avi to illustrate other children's books. Avi said he would also write a children's book if he could. His first book, *Things That Sometimes Happen*, was rejected by six publishers before it was accepted. He continued writing stories geared toward his sons, Kevin and Shaun, until he realized he enjoyed writing children's novels, especially historical fiction. In 1998 he combined a historical novel, ghost story, and science fiction story to create *Something Upstairs: A Tale of Ghosts*. He also wrote a contemporary humorous novel, *S.O.R. Losers*, and a coming-of-age novel, *Nothing but the Truth*, a Newbery honor book. His versatility in genre and style indicates his talent. He has won many awards including the Newbery Honor (1991) for *The True Confessions of Charlotte Doyle* and the Newbery Medal (2003) for *Crispin: The Cross of Lead*, which is also designated a 2003 Children's Choice for Advanced Readers by the International Reading Association.

Avi nas written over 40 children's books that are translated and published in more than ten countries. Several of his books have been adapted into plays, for radio shows, and into a film. Avi now writes full-time but continues to travel across the country, interacting with children, talking in schools, and discussing writing. He lives in Denver, Colorado, and his hobbies include reading, photography, and playing squash.

Major Characters

Crispin: protagonist; narrator and hero of the story, a.k.a. Asta's son; 13-year-old orphan serf in Stromford village ousted after being falsely accused of murder and theft

Bear: aka Orson Hrothgar; former monk now in disguise as an entertainer (jester, singer); a mentor to Crispin

John Aycliffe: antagonist; steward of the manor in Stromford; brother of Lady Furnival; searching for Crispin to kill him

Widow Daventry: tavern proprietor; close friend of Bear; protector of Crispin

Minor Characters

Asta: Crispin's mother; daughter of Lord Douglas; former mistress of Lord Furnival; dies at the beginning of the book

Goodwife Peregrine: oldest person in the village; gives Crispin food and warnings

Richard du Brey: courier sent with decree from Lady Furnival to kill Crispin

Cerdic: village boy; tricks Crispin and leads him into a trap

Father Quinel: priest of church in Stromford; helps Crispin

One-eyed Youth: boy from Lodgecot; spies on Crispin and reports his whereabouts to Aycliffe

Lord Furnival: knight, soldier, landowner, master of Great Wexly and surrounding villages; Crispin's father

Lady Furnival: wife of Lord Furnival; sister of John Aycliffe

John Ball: rebel leader; former priest who recruits peasants to revolt against lords (Note: John Ball was a real person who led a revolt in 1381 and was later executed for his efforts.)

Initiating Activities

1. Geography: Have students locate a map of the area from the 1300s to 1500s. Point out England, Scotland, Belgium, France, the Holy Lands, and Jerusalem. All of these locations are mentioned in the novel.

2. Research: To better understand *Crispin: The Cross of Lead*, check out books from the school and/or public libraries on the Middle Ages, the Plague, and life in medieval times. Use search engines to find Web sites to bookmark and make available for students. Have these references available throughout the study of the novel.

3. History: Discuss the Middle Ages with students. Have them create a time line as historical events are mentioned while reading the novel. Point out that the Middle Ages lasted for 1,000 years, and the time period covered in the novel is during the Late Middle Ages.

4. Art: Show pictures from books and Web sites depicting the time period of 1350–1400. If possible, show copies of primary sources—manuscripts, illustrations, paintings, tapestries, and drawings. Ask students to look at the cover of the book and predict what might happen in the story. Ask them to speculate on the purpose of the lead cross that Crispin holds.

5. Brainstorming: Have students draw an attribute web on the Middle Ages similar to the one below. Have students write the following eight topics on the eight spokes: 1. Slaves 2. Serfs/Peasants 3. Entertainers 4. Craftsmen 5. Merchants/Tradesmen 6. Members of the Clergy 7. Assistants to Nobles (steward, reeve, bailiff, soldier, etc.) 8. Knights & Lords. Divide the students into eight groups and assign each group one of the topics.

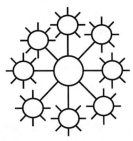

6. History/Science: Discuss the Plague (a.k.a. Black Plague, the Pestilence, Black Death, the Great Mortality, the Great Plague) of 1347–1349, its causes, its symptoms and effects, the approximate number of people who died, and the effects it had on the economy of the feudal system.

7. Social Studies: Discuss the role of the church in medieval times and the influence it had in the daily lives of peasants, including the tolling of bells to tell time and call people to prayer, holy days, and celebrations, etc. Also explain how the church leaders of the time required that fees be paid to them in order for a boy to study in a monastery to become a monk or priest.

8. Research: Discuss the author, Avi, and give information on his life, interests, and other works. Ask students to recall other books they have read by Avi and discuss the topics and themes of these books. Have students predict what will be in *Crispin: The Cross of Lead* based on what they know about the author.

Vocabulary Activities

1. Word Maps: Have students complete word maps like the one below for certain vocabulary words. For example: pauper (2), deigned (3), belied (66), abated (90), mollify (120), timorous (145), fervor (177), succumb (229), disdain (240), unfettered (262).

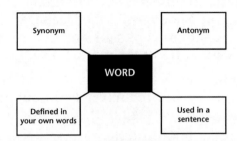

2. Medieval Math: Have students analyze vocabulary words with mathematical meanings. Examples for measurement include: leagues (24), rod (49). Examples of money include: farthing (12), shillings (41). Encourage students to look for other mathematical words in the text as they read. Have them find pictures of the coins and information about their worth in books, dictionaries, or on the Internet.

3. Agriculture Words: Have students analyze vocabulary words relating to agriculture. Examples include: fallow (18), crofts (19), sowing (20), millrace (46).

4. Antiquated Vocabulary: Have students develop a set of 3" x 5" cards of words indicative of the Middle Ages and not often used in modern times. Put the word on one side and a short definition on the other side. Give students an envelope or baggie to store the cards for use throughout the unit. Examples, excluding the words listed in #2 and #3 above, include: villeins (12), serfs (12), cottar (14), wattle (15), daub (18), henceforward (77), guildhalls (77), mummers (84), bade (112), beseech (125), lest (129), portcullis (144), solars (149), kirtle (151), pattens (151). Encourage students to look for other antiquated words not included on their vocabulary lists.

5. Medieval Mimics: Have students act out, mime, or represent vocabulary words for other students to guess. Examples include: astride (2), transfixed (8), genuflected (29), lurching (55), prudence (65), agape (90), nimbly (170), caterwauling (194), succumb (229), skittered (259).

6. Multiple Meanings: Have students learn new meanings for common words used in an unusual way in the novel, such as: run (18), lime (28), font (28), rents (64), rushes (151).

7. Suffix Hint: Have students find words in the text with the suffix, -ous (possessing the qualities of). Examples include: punctilious (83), timorous (145), portentous (147), scabrous (225). Have students take other words from the book, add the suffix -ous, and redefine the word. Have them note how the part of speech changes to an adjective when the suffix is added. Examples to use include: tumult (46), dire (52).

8. Vocabulary Sort: Have students sort vocabulary words into categories (e.g., nouns, verbs, adjectives, adverbs, conjunctions).

9. Sentences: Have students select three to four vocabulary words from each section of the novel and use them in one sentence. Examples from Chapters 33–34: press (143), palpable (146), din (146). The potential danger from the press of the crowd was palpable, so we hastily moved inside away from the din.

10. Interesting Adjectives: Have students complete word maps like the one below for vocabulary words in the novel. Examples are: cloying (5), tolling (13), rasping (40), palpable (146), serpentine (174), vulnerable (184), fragmentary (221), vaulted (247).

Word Map

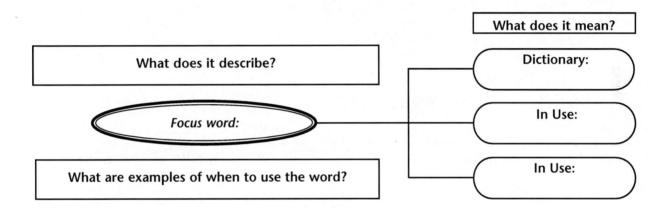

What does it mean?

What does it describe?

Dictionary:

Focus word:

In Use:

What are examples of when to use the word?

In Use:

Story Map

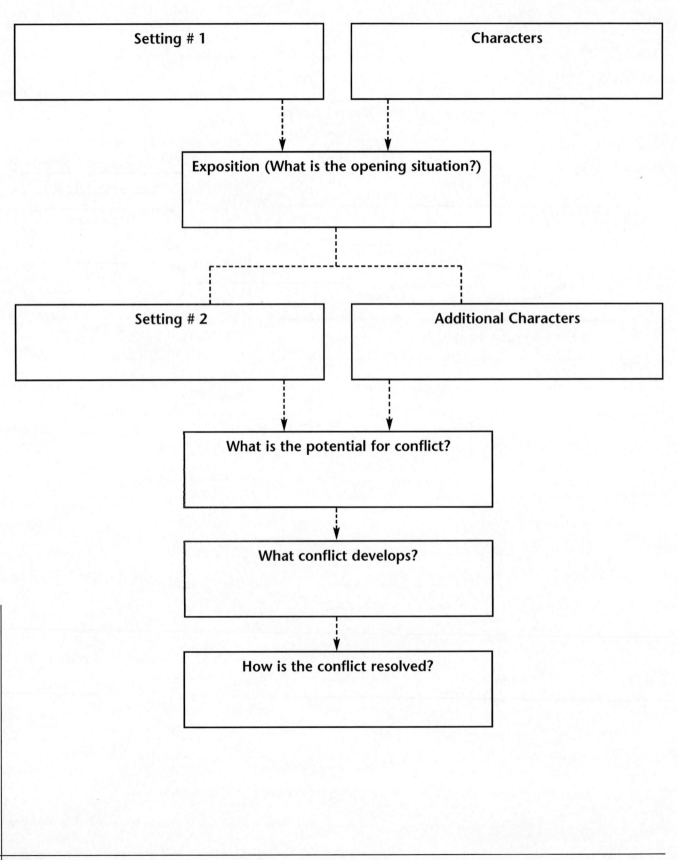

Setting # 1

Characters

Exposition (What is the opening situation?)

Setting # 2

Additional Characters

What is the potential for conflict?

What conflict develops?

How is the conflict resolved?

Feelings

Directions: Choose a character from the book and complete the chart below.

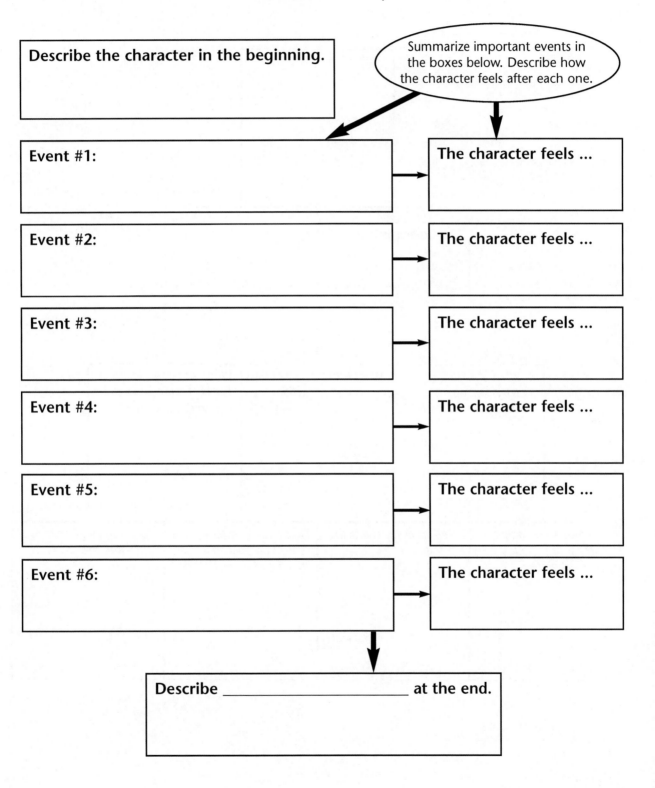

Describe the character in the beginning.

Summarize important events in the boxes below. Describe how the character feels after each one.

Event #1:

The character feels ...

Event #2:

The character feels ...

Event #3:

The character feels ...

Event #4:

The character feels ...

Event #5:

The character feels ...

Event #6:

The character feels ...

Describe _____ at the end.

Character Analysis Blocks

Directions: Select a character from the book to describe using the blocks below.

Who is the character?			

What does the character do?	Why does s/he do it?

What, if anything, is significant about the character's name?	What is the nature of this character's actions? (reactive, active, important, consequential, secondary)	What is the significance of the book's time and place to the character?

What is unusual or important about the character?	How does the character change in the story?	Does the character remind you of another character from another book? Who?	Do you know anyone similar to this character?

Metaphors and Similes

A **metaphor** is a comparison between two unlike objects. For example, "he was a human tree." A **simile** is a comparison between two unlike objects that uses the words *like* or *as*. For example, "the color of her eyes was like the cloudless sky."

Directions: Complete the chart below by listing metaphors and similes from the novel, as well as the page numbers on which they are found. Identify metaphors with an "M" and similes with an "S." Translate the comparisons in your own words, and then list the objects being compared.

Metaphors/Similes	Ideas/Objects Being Compared
1. Translation:	
2. Translation:	
3. Translation:	

Chapter 1, pp. 1–5

A poor boy is orphaned after the death of his mother, Asta. Father Quinel helps Asta's son with funeral-arrangements. The evil steward of the manor, John Aycliffe, informs Asta's son that he must deliver his ox to the manor as payment for his mother's death. Asta's son becomes overwhelmed.

Vocabulary
shroud (1)
pauper (2)
steward (2)
astride (2)
deigned (3)
transgression (3)
poaching (3)
forfeit (3)
manor (4)
tunic (4)
bracken (5)

Discussion Questions

1. Why didn't the village people in the fields kneel as a sign of respect when the priest and Asta's son passed by with his mother's wrapped body? (*When Asta was alive, she and her son were shunned and taunted by the villagers. pp. 1–2*)

2. Why was Asta buried with her feet facing east? (*Asta's body points toward Jerusalem, which is east of England, based on a belief that God would return to the holy city of Jerusalem where buried Christians would rise up and join each other. p. 2*)

3. What can you tell about John Aycliffe's character? Why do you think so? (*Answers will vary. He is mean and demanding. He frowns, scowls, kicks, speaks harshly, whips, imprisons, and executes. p. 3*)

4. Why does Asta's son plunge into the woods? (*He is frightened, sad, in despair, afraid, distressed, and worried about his life. pp. 4–5*)

5. What is the meaning of this sentence, "In the midst of life comes death, in the midst of death comes life" (p. 1)? (*Answers will vary.*)

6. **Prediction:** What will Asta's son do after he gives up his ox and can no longer work in the fields?

Supplementary Activities

1. Writing: Have students brainstorm what they know about the Middle Ages. Discuss. As they read, students should determine whether their perceptions are accurate.

2. Social Studies: Describe the death tax to students. When a serf died, the family had to pay a death tax to the lord of the manor because the lord considered it a monetary loss to lose a worker. Have students research death taxes and how they affected the serfs in medieval times.

3. Drama: Group students in threes. One will be Asta's son, one Aycliffe, and one Father Quinel. Have them stage the scene on pages 3–4 of the novel with the three characters. Encourage students to use appropriate non-verbal expressions to enhance the scene.

4. Literary Analysis: Have students begin the Story Map on page 8 of this guide.

Chapter 2, pp. 5–10

Asta's son is lost in the deep woods. He is cold and wet. He sees a fluttering torch and hears voices. He creeps close and sees Aycliffe and a well-dressed stranger with a parchment document containing what seems to be dangerous information. When the two men notice Asta's son, they chase after him, but Asta's son escapes when he falls off a small cliff.

Vocabulary
cloying (5)
welt (6)
murk (6)
minions (6)
parchment (7)
affixed (7)
transfixed (8)
avail (8)
engulfed (10)

Discussion Questions

1. What scares Asta's son about the night? (*There may be outlaws, wolves, or even the devil out at night. p. 6*)

2. What did Asta mean when she said, "Curiosity is another name for Satan" (p. 6)? (*Being inquisitive may lead to trouble and harm.*)

3. How can you tell the stranger is a gentleman? (*his dress—a long cape and hood over a blue, quilted tunic with yellow shiny clasps; also his "fine head of a horse," p. 7*)

4. Why would Aycliffe care if Asta's son saw the stranger and heard them talking? (*Answers will vary. pp. 7–8*)

5. **Prediction:** What do you think is written on the parchment?

6. **Prediction:** Will Asta's son return to his village?

Supplementary Activities

1. Character Analysis: Have students use the chart on page 9 of this guide to analyze a character in the novel. Students should continue their charts as they read.

2. Literary Analysis: **Plot Development**—Have students begin a 3-column list titled "Foreshadowing." In one column write "Foreshadow," in the next "Page Number," and in the third column write "What May Happen." Point out the scene on page 8 of the novel when Aycliffe and the gentleman talk in the woods. Ask students what the conversation may mean and what it tells about the story's development. Students should add to their foreshadowing chart as they read the book.

3. Social Studies: Discuss the role the church played in the everyday lives of people in the Middle Ages. Point out the many religious references in this chapter.

4. Literary Analysis: **Alliteration**—Introduce the definition and examples of alliteration. Students should begin a list of alliterations, starting with "murk and midnight" (p. 6). Instruct students to add to their lists of alliteration as they read the book.

Chapter 3, pp. 10–13

Asta's son tells of his background, his birth, his parents, the villagers, the times, the church, and his feelings.

Vocabulary
jibes (11)
embedded (11)
villeins (12)
serfs (12)
mercenary (12)
farthing (12)

Discussion Questions

1. Why does Asta's son feel he "existed in a shadow" (p. 10)? (*He does not know his father's name; he is very poor and has few friends. pp. 10–11*)

2. What does Asta's son mean when he says, "We were not slaves. But neither were we free" (p. 12)? (*They were serfs bound to work on Lord Fumival's land. They had no other place to live or earn money.*)

3. Do you feel Asta's son's pessimistic tone is justified? Why or why not? (*Answers will vary. pp. 12–13*)

4. What can Asta's son do to change his life? (*Answers will vary. pp. 12–13*)

5. **Prediction:** Will Asta's son continue to live as a serf in Stromford?

Supplementary Activities

1. Social Studies: Ask a volunteer to look up information on St. Giles—who he was, what he did, when he lived, and what day St. Giles' Day is celebrated.

2. Social Studies: Show a video or prepare a presentation on The Plague/Black Death, 1347–1349.

3. Social Studies/Critical Thinking: Have students research medieval laws regarding serfs and/or villeins. Discuss the concept of the lord (not the serfs) owning the land. Explain how the serfs were bound by law to the lord. Compare and contrast this to slavery in the United States, prior to the Civil War.

4. Writing: Students should respond to this prompt: How does Asta's son perceive himself? They must give examples from Chapter 3 to support their opinions.

Chapter 4, pp. 13–19

Asta's son returns to the village and his cottage only to find the bailiff and reeve tearing down his home. He flees to a high rock in the forest.

Vocabulary
tolling (13)
untoward (14)
cottar (14)
reeve (15)
wattle (15)
ford (17)
trestle (17)
run (18)
daub (18)
commons (18)
fallow (18)
crofts (19)

Discussion Questions

1. How would you describe Asta's cottage? (*Set off from the village, it is a rented, one room dwelling with a thin thatch roof and a dirt floor made of wattle and clay. pp. 14–15*)

2. How does Asta's son tell time? (*by the sun's position and the church bells, pp. 14–16*)

3. Why does the steward want Asta's cottage destroyed? (*Answers will vary. p. 15*)

4. How would you judge Asta's son's viewpoint of his village? (*Answers will vary, but should indicate that he is fond of his village. pp. 16–19*)

5. What do the villagers gain from working so hard for the lord? (*protection from enemies and the "hope of heaven," p. 19*)

6. **Prediction:** Will enemies attack the village?

Supplementary Activities

1. Social Studies: Have students research the tolling of church bells to call the people to prayer and list related words, mentioned in this section and the last section—Compline (p. 5), Prime (p. 14), and Terce (p. 16).

2. Social Studies: Have students find pictures of huts with thatch, wattle, and daub. They should mark off a 6-foot by 15-foot section of the classroom to represent the size of a small medieval cottage.

3. Social Studies/Critical Thinking: Draw a Venn diagram on the board, and have students compare and contrast the book's descriptions of the manor (pp. 17–18) and the peasants' cottages (pp. 18–19).

Chapters 5–7, pp. 20–26

While Asta's son is hiding in the woods, the priest calls the villagers to the church to hear important news from Aycliffe and the gentleman stranger. Villagers are recruited and armed to search for Asta's son. Asta's son overhears the pursuers say he is accused of breaking into the manor house and stealing money. They do not believe he did and quietly complain about Aycliffe. Asta's son, alarmed and discouraged, plans to seek help from the priest later that night.

Vocabulary
sowing (20)
pealing (20)
canonical (20)
glaives (22)
hue and cry (22)
archer (23)
leagues (24)
moot (25)

Discussion Questions

1. How does Asta's son describe himself in his prayer? Choose one word to describe what he is feeling. (*He has no name, feels he is nothing, does not know what to do, feels all alone, and thinks he is full of sin. Answers will vary, but may include desperate or depressed. p. 21*)

2. Why does Asta's son want to go to the priest for help? Can he trust him? Why or why not? (*The priest is the only person Asta's son can trust because his mother trusted him, and the priest returned their trust with kindness. Answers will vary. p. 22*)

3. A "hue and cry" is a loud exclamation to announce pursuit of a felon. Who has the hue and cry been raised against? What would you do in this situation? (*Asia's son. Answers will vary. pp. 22–23*)

4. Why does Asta's son feel he was not caught by the search party? (*He believes the "merciful saints" were kind to him. p. 23*)

5. How do Matthew and Luke feel about Asta's son? (*They don't think he committed the crime and is far away by now. pp. 23–25*)

6. How do Matthew and Luke feel about Aycliffe the steward? (*They are bitter about the things the steward has done—increased their labors, imposed countless fines, taken many taxes, and increased punishments. p. 25*)

7. Do you think it is treason to speak against one's government and/or leaders? Why or why not? (*Answers will vary. pp. 25–26*)

8. **Prediction:** Will the search party catch Asta's son when he goes to see the priest?

Supplementary Activities

1. Drama: Pair students and ask them to re-read Matthew and Luke's conversation on pages 23–25 of the novel. Have students act out the dialogue.

2. Math: Research the measurement of a league (p. 24 of the novel). About how many leagues do you live from school?

3. Literary Analysis: Similes and Metaphors—Using the chart on page 11 of this guide, have students begin a list of metaphors and similes that they will add to as they read the book.

Chapter 8, pp. 27–36

Asta's son seeks Father Quinel for help. Asta's son tells him of the meeting he saw in the woods, and the priest tells him the gentleman stranger is Richard du Brey, a messenger for Lord Furnival. Asta's son learns he has been declared a wolf's head, an outlaw that can be killed by anyone. The priest warns him to flee to save his life and tells him his real name is Crispin. The priest urges Crispin to hide in a city or an abbey. The priest also reveals to Crispin that his mother could read and write. Father Quinel asks to see Crispin the next night to give him food and tell him more about his father before Crispin flees the village.

Vocabulary

alb (27)
wizened (27)
tonsured (27)
tallow (28)
lime (28)
font (28)
genuflected (29)
wolf's head (31)

Discussion Questions

1. How does Father Quinel feel about Asta's son coming to see him? Should Crispin trust the priest? (*The priest hopes Crispin will come, knows that he has not committed the theft, wants to help him, and gives him a blessing. Answers will vary. pp. 27–32*)

2. Why is Crispin hesitant to leave Stromford? (*He has never been away from his village, does not know where to go, has no money, and is alone. pp. 31–36*)

3. Why was Asta secretive about Crispin's name, his father, and the fact that she could read and write? (*Answers will vary. pp. 31–35*)

4. Why does Crispin respond to the priest, "Freedom?...What has that to do with me?" (p. 32)? (*Answers will vary. p. 32*)

5. Why does the priest insist on waiting to tell Crispin more about his father? (*Father Quinel feels Crispin will be safer if he does not know until just before leaving Stromford. p. 34*)

6. What is the importance of the cross of lead? (*It has writing on it and may tell Crispin more about his mother and father. p. 35*)

7. **Prediction:** Does anyone notice when Crispin leaves the church?

Supplementary Activities

1. Social Studies: Show a picture of a monk or priest with tonsured hair, a wool robe with a cowl, a rope around the waist, and a cross around his neck.

2. Social Studies: Have students research the medieval laws of claiming sanctuary (p. 28) and the wolf's head reward (p. 31).

3. Writing: Ask students to respond in their journals and describe how Asta's son must feel when he learns his real name is Crispin, a high-born name, and that his mother could read and write. Students should also address how Crispin feels that his mother kept this information secret.

Chapters 9–13, pp. 37–54

Crispin goes to the church, but a village boy called Cerdic meets him, instead of Father Quinel. Crispin learns from Goodwife Peregrine that the reward for killing him is 20 shillings. Cerdic leads Crispin into a trap at the mill, but Crispin escapes. He discovers that Father Quinel was killed. Crispin wanders through the forest in shock and sees the steward and bailiff searching for him.

Vocabulary
crone (39)
foreboding (40)
rasping (40)
shillings (41)
disquiet (42)
proper (43)
millrace (46)
tumult (46)
albeit (48)
rod (49)
lanced (50)
dire (52)

Discussion Questions

1. How would you describe Goodwife Peregrine? (*She is the oldest person in the village; has a special wisdom for healing, midwifery, and magic; is tiny, stooped, and has a red mark on her right cheek. pp. 38–40*)

2. How do you know Aycliffe is desperate for Crispin to be killed? Why do you think Crispin's death is so important to Aycliffe? (*He has fabricated Crispin's crimes and is offering a 20-shilling reward, a half year's wages, for Crispin's capture or death. p. 41*)

3. What happens as Crispin and Cerdic approach the mill? (*Cerdic leads him into a trap where eight men are hiding with weapons. The men beat a drum to confuse Crispin. pp. 44–45*)

4. Why does Crispin run back toward the village? (*He can't swim and is scared of the river. p. 47*)

5. What happened to Father Quinel? Why do you think this happened? (*His throat was slit and he is dead. Answers will vary, but may include that he helped Crispin. pp. 48–49*)

6. What does Crispin beg for in his prayers? (*mercy, guidance, comfort and protection, blessing on the priest and himself, pp. 48–50*)

7. Why does Crispin stay close to the road where he is more likely to be seen? (*He does not want to lose his connection with his village, as he has never ventured so far from it before in his life. He is fearful of his future and the unknown. p. 52*)

8. What spurns Crispin on? (*what Father Quinel told him to do—get far from Stromford to a city or town that has its own liberties, p. 53*)

9. Why does Crispin no longer wish to live? (*He misses his mother and feels defeated as he lives in secrecy. pp. 53–54*)

10. What does Crispin's prayer reveal about his character? (*Answers will vary. Suggestion—He is humble and aware of his faults. He seems to feel lonely and abandoned, but he is confident enough to pray for a place in Heaven. pp. 53–54*)

11. **Prediction:** Will Crispin be seen on the road?

Supplementary Activities

1. Literary Analysis: **Similes**—Examples: "like a new garment that replaces an old" garment (p. 37) and "herbs that hung from the rafters look like dangling carcasses" (p. 40).

2. Literary Analysis/Alliteration: Have students add to their lists. Example: "the sudden silences that suggested something lurking near" (p. 50).

3. Art: Have students sketch a picture of Goodwife Peregrine as described on pages 39–42 of the novel.

4. Social Studies: Have students research mills and millraces of medieval times and how they were used to grind wheat and barley. They should also research boundary crosses, one of which was placed at each of the four cardinal directions (N, E, S, W) in most medieval villages.

5. Writing: Have students respond in their journals about a time they were lost or homesick, as Crispin is in Chapter 13.

Chapters 14–15, pp. 54–60

On his third day of escape, Crispin sees a hanged man, which renews his strength to fight his own death. He continues in a westerly direction and finds a village similar to his own, but no one lives there. Only skeletons remain from the devastation of the Plague.

Vocabulary
lurching (55)
distended (55)
pillaged (56)
dell (57)
hamlet (57)
trepidation (58)
pestilence (59)
blight (59)

Discussion Questions

1. What do you think is written on the paper affixed to the hanged man? (*Answers will vary. p. 55*)

2. How does seeing the corpse affect Crispin? (*He thinks it is a sign from God sent as a warning. He decides he wants to live. pp. 55–56*)

3. What does Crispin mean whe he sees the abandoned village and says his "skin crawled with trepidation" (p. 58)? (*Answers will vary.*)

4. What does Crispin believe caused the Great Plague? (*God sent it as a punishment for people's sins. p. 59*)

5. What does Crispin do to protect himself in the village? Do you believe these things will protect him? (*He prays and grips the cross of lead. Answers will vary. p. 59*)

6. **Prediction:** After hearing the singing, will Crispin flee the village, or will he investigate?

Supplementary Activities

1. Literary Analysis: **Descriptive Language**—Have one student read the first paragraph of Chapter 14 aloud in order for the class to hear the descriptive language.

2. Science: Review the Plague and the causes of the disease between 1347–1349.

Chapter 16, pp. 60–66

Crispin hears someone singing in the abandoned village and finds a large man dressed in colorful clothes. The man teases Crispin, asks him many questions, and tricks him.

Vocabulary
ruddy (61)
bollock (62)
rents (64)
cur (64)
doddering (64)
parliaments (65)
venison (65)
sweetmeats (65)
prudence (65)
belied (66)

Discussion Questions

1. Why does Crispin not tell the man where he is from? (*He does not know or trust the man, and he is afraid the man might kill him for the wolf's head reward. pp. 63–64*)

2. What is your impression of the man in the church? (*Answers will vary. pp. 62–65*)

3. The author employs humorous moments in the conversation between the meeting of Crispin and the man in the church. Discuss the ways the readers know parts of the conversation are meant to be humorous. (*Answers will vary.*)

4. How does the man feel about the king and officials of the kingdom? (*He does not think well of them—the king is senile, the officials are corrupt, and they are all tyrants. pp. 63–64*)

5. Do you think the man is committing treason to speak of officials in this way? (*Answers will vary. Note: Connect the students' responses to what they said about Matthew and Luke's discussion in Chapter 7, page 65.*)

6. Discuss the meaning of tyranny and give examples. Relate it to the man's opinion of the king on pages 64–65 of the novel. (*Discussions will vary.*)

7. The man says the king's motto is, "It is as it is." What does this mean? What would your motto be if you were king? (*It means the king is satisfied with the way things are and does not wish for anything to change. Answers will vary. p. 65*)

8. Contrast the mottos, "It is as it is" and "Let it be as it may be." With which motto do you most agree? (*Answers will vary. Note that the second motto heralds change while the first does not. p. 65*)

9. **Prediction:** Will the man harm Crispin or turn him in to Aycliffe?

Supplementary Activities

1. Music: Find music and ballads of the medieval period. Play them for the class as a focus for this chapter.

2. Art: Have students make a sketch of the singing man Crispin finds in the abandoned village as described on pages 61–62 of the novel.

3. Geography: Show a map of Europe and have students find Italy and Belgium (referred to as Flemish) as mentioned on page 65 of the novel. Then have students research why the term "Flemish" is used to refer to these areas.

Chapters 17–19, pp. 66–80

The man grabs Crispin by the wrist and demands an explanation of why Crispin is there. He claims Crispin as his servant. The man demonstrates his talent for juggling, tells of his travels, and reveals his name, Orson Hrothgar or Bear.

Vocabulary

mockingly (67)
putrid (69)
screed (70)
pate (74)
surname (76)
henceforward (77)
wend (77)
revels (77)
guildhalls (77)

Discussion Questions

1. What does the man mean when he says, "Bread is never free, boy"? (*Answers mil vary, but may include the idea that one cannot get something without some kind of payment or favor. p. 66*)

2. How does the man feel about priests and the church? (*He mocks them as he did the king and the officials. p. 67*)

3. Why does the man say Crispin must become his servant? (*There is an English law that allows a person who unlawfully leaves his/her true master to be claimed as a servant by the first free man who finds him/her. p. 69*)

4. Why does the man make Crispin take a pledge of loyalty and service to him? (*Answers will vary but may include the man wants to control Crispin, scare Crispin, or keep Crispin from escaping. pp. 70–71*)

5. The man believes that "some day none of us will have masters" (p. 72). How does Crispin react to this idea? (*Crispin cannot respond because he is surprised by the man's argument for living in a world without masters. pp. 72–73*)

6. How does the man earn a living? (*He goes to towns and cities, juggling and entertaining people who pay him. p. 77*)

7. Why does the man laugh when Crispin tells him that he can follow an ox, sow seed, gather crops, and thresh wheat and barley? (*The man does not think those skills are worth much in a city. p. 77*)

8. What does Crispin mean when he says, "I wanted to gain my liberty" (p. 78)? (*Father Quinel told Crispin if he could live in a city or town free of a master for one year and a day, he would become a free man. Because Bear has claimed him, he is no longer free of a master. Chapter 8 and p. 78*)

9. Do you think "Bear" is a good name for Orson Hrothgar? Why or why not? (*Answers will vary. p. 79*)

10. What does Bear mean when he says, "Large things are brewing...Our task is to stay alive and measure this great kingdom with our feet, our eyes, our ears" (pp. 79–80)? (*Answers will vary, but should include reference to Bear being a part of a plan to cause change in the way the feudal system works.*)

11. **Prediction:** Will Bear and Crispin make it to Great Wexly?

Supplementary Activities

1. Writing: Have students note the "words of wisdom" given by the man on page 66 of the novel when he says, "Bread is never free, boy." In their journals, have students list examples of words of wisdom, warning, and advice given to them by their parents, grandparents, teachers, etc.

2. Social Studies: Discuss "treason" and examples of famous historical figures who committed treason.

3. Geography: Locate Scotland, Gascony (southwestern France), and Brittany (northwestern France), on a map of Europe.

4. Social Studies: Have students research the market fairs held in the Middle Ages and how "fair coins" (p. 77) came about. Have students present their findings to the class or stage a market fair of their own for the entire class, grade, or school to enjoy.

Chapters 20–23, pp. 80–95

Bear and Crispin travel through the countryside, and Bear reveals more of his life story. He teaches Crispin how to juggle and play the recorder, but ties Crispin to a tree while he searches for food. Bear tells more of his riotous life and asks Crispin more about his parents.

Vocabulary
punctilious (83)
willy-nilly (83)
acolyte (83)
mummers (84)
beguiled (84)
faltered (85)
jeopardy (89)
stoke (90)
agape (90)
abated (90)

Discussion Questions

1. As a class, define irony and discuss the irony in Bear taking Crispin as a servant. (*On one hand, Bear says he hates tyranny where one person has absolute control. On the other hand, he claims Crispin as his servant. p. 80*)

2. Should Crispin trust Bear? Why doesn't he run away from him? (*Answers will vary. Because Crispin swore a sacred oath to be Bear's servant, even though it was by force, he is afraid of the consequences if he breaks the oath. p. 81*)

3. What does Bear reveal about his past? (*Bear's father paid fees to a Benedictine abbey in York to take Bear in at age 12. He studied to be a priest but then ran off and joined a group of mummers for ten years. Later he was a soldier. pp. 83–85*)

4. What is the penalty for poaching if the hunter is caught? What does Bear mean when he says, "That's the kind of freedom that exists in this kingdom" (p. 89)? (*death; Answers will vary, but may include that Bear is being sarcastic because people are not free if they are so hungry they must hunt on the landowners' land for food, only to be killed if they catch something that could help them survive. p. 89*)

5. What does Bear think about Lord Furnival? Why do you think so? (*He does not think well of him because he says Furnival is arrogant, fights poorly, brags, drinks, kills, loots, is cruel to prisoners, and is a womanizer. pp. 91–92*)

6. Why does Crispin find comfort in telling Bear about his troubles? (*Crispin is relieved to have someone listen to him. p. 94*)

7. **Prediction:** Will Bear betray Crispin to Lord Furnival's men when they arrive in Great Wexly?

Supplementary Activities

1. Social Studies/Drama: Tell students about mummers (p. 84), masked performers who performed plays and dances in the Middle Ages. Ask students to find out more about them and what type of plays they performed, or have students stage a play or dance that a mummer in the Middle Ages might have performed.

2. Music: Have students look at the lyrics on page 87 of the novel. Have them research music of the fourteenth century and play recordings of this type of music for the class.

3. Writing: Have students read the last paragraph on page 90 of the novel and the last paragraph on page 92 of the novel and comment on their descriptive nature. Ask them to pick a time in their own lives and write a short paragraph or poem about it using similar descriptive language.

4. Literary Analysis/Foreshadowing: Have students add to their foreshadowing list. (Crispin reveals how his mother sometimes held him, but was repulsed by him at other times. p. 94)

Chapters 24–27, pp. 95–114

Bear gives Crispin advice about how to live life and challenges Crispin's basic beliefs. (Note: The main themes of the novel are highlighted in Chapters 24–25.) Crispin practices playing the recorder in order to assist Bear in entertaining in a nearby town. As they approach the village of Burley, they see John Aycliffe with 12 men by the bridge as if waiting for someone.

Vocabulary
mirth (97)
livery (97)
heretic (100)
sham (106)
aloft (109)
spinney (111)
summit (111)
bade (112)
emblazoned (112)
paled (113)

Discussion Questions

1. What does Bear mean when he says, "Lose your sorrows and you'll find your freedom" (p. 97)? (*Answers will vary.*)

2. Why does Crispin feel he is only bad and not good? Do you agree or disagree with him? Why or why not? (*Answers will vary. Suggestion—He thinks sin is imbedded inside of him since so many terrible things have happened to him. Because of his religious upbringing, he may feel God is punishing him for bad things he has done. p. 97*)

3. What does Bear mean when he says, "living by answers is a form of death. It's only questions that keep you living" (pp. 97–98)? (*Answers will vary, but may include that curiosity, reflection, doubting, seeking the truth, etc., help one have a better life.*)

4. What does Bear mean when he says, "[your cross is] useless…God is near…He needs no special words or objects to approach Him…churches, priests—they're all unneeded. The only cross you need is the one in your heart" (p. 99)? Why is this statement important to the story? What does this statement have to do with the theme of freedom? (*Answers will vary, but may include the idea that no emissaries are required to communicate directly with God. Bear is challenging one of Crispin's most deeply-held beliefs with this statement. p. 99*)

5. What does Bear mean by "…he who knows a bit of everything knows nothing. But he who knows a little bit well, know much of all" (p. 100)? Do you agree or disagree with Bear's statement? (*Answers will vary.*)

6. Do you agree or disagree with Bear's idea that every person should be his or her own master? Explain your point of view. (*Answers will vary. p. 101*)

7. Discuss the term paradox and apply the term to Bear. Think of other people you know who seem to display a paradoxical nature. (*Answers will vary. pp. 97, 103*)

8. Why does Crispin think he does not have a soul? What is a "soul"? (*He has never felt it. Answers will vary. p. 106*)

9. How does the music and dancing affect Crispin? Discuss the importance of the arts (music, poetry, painting, writing, etc.) in daily life. (*He is amazed he learns to play the recorder and astonished that Bear dances so well. He is pleased with his progress and the thought of making money by entertaining people. pp. 108–109*)

10. What do the pigeons signal to Bear? (*Their swirling about the sky makes Bear realize something is agitating them. This clue causes Bear to cautiously creep up a hill to look ahead. p. 111*)

11. Why are the soldiers on the road at the bridge? (*Answers will vary, but should include the idea that they are waiting to catch Crispin as he heads to Great Wexly. pp. 112–113*)

12. Discuss freedom, self-determination, and self-reliance as presented in these chapters. Where does the author address each theme? What is he trying to communicate about each theme? How does the author develop the characters to help him communicate these? (*Answers will vary. Note how Bear is critical to challenge Crispin's ideas about freedom, self-determination, and self-reliance.*)

13. **Prediction:** Will the soldiers catch Crispin?

Supplementary Activities

1. Literary Analysis: **Oxymorons**—Ask students to read the phrase on page 107 of the novel, "rough kindness," and tell why it is an oxymoron. Have students brainstorm other examples such as "deafening silence," "terribly happy," and "foolishly wise."

2. Literary Analysis: Have students update their lists of similes, metaphors, alliteration, humor, and words of wisdom with examples from these chapters.

Chapters 28–32, pp. 114–138

Bear and Crispin take a different direction in their travels to protect Crispin from Aycliffe. Bear reads the inscription on Crispin's lead cross but does not reveal what it says. The pair entertains the villagers at Lodgecot and earns some money. There they hear of a notorious murderer on the loose. A one-eyed youth in the crowd seems suspicious of them. Bear asks Crispin to become his apprentice rather than his servant. Crispin becomes a free person.

Vocabulary
subdued (118)
mollify (120)
wry (122)
snuffling (124)
penance (125)
beseech (125)
mazer (126)
gambols (127)
dexterity (127)
malevolence (128)
lest (129)
courier (130)
enraptured (133)
apprentice (138)

Discussion Questions

1. Why does Crispin think Bear found meaning in the writing on his lead cross? What do you think is inscribed on the cross? (*Bear squints to read it closely, but then refuses to tell Crispin what it says. Answers wil vary. pp. 117–118*)

2. Bear says he is part of a brotherhood to make things better and to bring about change. What does he mean by this? (*Answers will vary, but students should recognize that Bear's business with a man in Great Wexly is related to the brotherhood. It can also be assumed that Bear's brotherhood is opposed to the current type of government and government officials. p. 120*)

3. Why does Bear avoid telling Crispin what is written on his cross? (*Bear is afraid for Crispin and believes what it says may put Crispin in danger. pp. 121–122*)

4. Why does Bear tell the Lodgecot priest that Crispin is his son? (*in order to protect Crispin and his identity, p. 125*)

5. To whom does the priest alert Bear? How does Bear respond? Why does he respond as he does? (*Crispin; He thanks the priest for the warning and says he would like to earn the 20-shilling reward for the wolf's head. Answers will vary. pp. 129–130*)

6. Why does Bear give Crispin a penny? (*Crispin worked hard entertaining the people, and Bear feels Crispin has earned a portion of their payments. He also wants to stress to Crispin that they are now free. p. 133*)

7. What is Bear's advice to Crispin about speaking boldly to everyone? Why does he want Crispin to behave this way? (*He tells Crispin to look people in the eyes when he speaks to them and to be more confident in who he is. Answers will vary. pp. 135–136*)

8. Why does Bear equate Lord Furnival with the devil? (*Bear has seen how badly the people are treated and how miserable they are. He blames these conditions on Furnival's tyranny. p. 137*)

9. In what ways does Bear show Crispin he cares about him? (*Answers will vary but should include the bluntness with which Bear tells Crispin he cares for him, and how he asks Crispin to become his apprentice rather than his servant. pp. 137–138*)

10. Do you think Crispin should trust Bear? (*Answers will vary. p. 138*)

Supplementary Activities

1. Drama: Have students volunteer to act out the scene on pages 125–130 of the novel in Lodgecot where Crispin and Bear perform. Students not playing the parts of the priest, Bear, Crispin, and the one-eyed youth can be villagers and children in the audience.

2. Social Studies: Have students research the Feast of Saint John the Baptist and Midsummer Day to find out more of what Crispin and Bear will see and do in Great Wexly.

3. Literary Analysis/Flashback: Have students relate the mention of the courier du Brey on page 130 of the novel with what happened on page 7 (Chapter 2).

4. Writing: Ask students to write a journal entry regarding why Crispin is "enraptured by the notion that we were indeed free" (p. 133).

5. Social Studies/Writing: Have students research the pros and cons of being an apprentice compared to being a serf. Have students write a one-page persuasive paper on why one is better than the other.

Chapters 33–34, pp. 139–150

As Bear and Crispin approach Great Wexly they see more and more people, including pilgrims, tradesmen, merchants, and soldiers. Crispin is in awe of the city and new sights but is also frightened of the many soldiers and the filth in the city. They go to the Green Man tavern to stay.

Vocabulary
pilgrim (139)
tinkers (141)
press (143)
portcullis (144)
gauntlet (145)
timorous (145)
palpable (146)
din (146)
portentous (147)
cacophony (147)
swill (147)
solars (149)

Discussions Questions

1. Why does Bear describe all of the people to Crispin? (*Bear knows Crispin has not seen any of these types of people before and is probably curious p. 139*)

2. Why does Crispin say, "it was not just words I had to learn to read, but what people wore as well" (p. 142)? Do you think it is as important to be able to "read" what people wear today as it was for Crispin? Why or why not? (*He realizes that people's clothing tells much about their livelihood, wealth, education, and upbringing. Answers will vary. pp. 139–142*)

3. Why do the people squeeze together as they enter the city? (*In order to enter the city, the people must pass through a tunnel at the Bishop's Gate. pp. 143–144*)

4. Why is black cloth wrapped around the shield above the gate? (*Answers will vary, but hopefully students will guess it tells of someone's death or funeral. p. 144*)

5. Do you think the soldiers at the gate are looking for Crispin? Why or why not? (*Answers will vary. pp. 146–147*)

6. What assaults Crispin inside the city? (*the large number of people, the noise, the stench, the animals, and the crowded buildings, pp. 147–148*)

7. What realization hits Crispin about his own village, Stromford? (*He realizes how very poor his village is. pp. 149–150*)

8. **Prediction:** What is Bear's dangerous business?

Supplementary Activities

1. Geography: On a map of Europe, have students point out Avignon and Jerusalem (p. 140).

2. Social Studies: Have students research the skills and lifestyles of tradesmen, traders, tinkers, masons, carpenters, doctors, lawyers, and apothecaries of the time period as mentioned on page 141 of the novel.

3. Art: Have students draw with map colors or markers what Crispin describes on page 143 of the novel when he sees the wall and spires of the city.

Chapters 35–37, pp. 150–163

Widow Daventry, a good friend of Bear's, runs the Green Man tavern. They learn Lord Furnival died two weeks ago. They stay in a room on the second floor that also has a special hidden room. Crispin sneaks outside to see more of the city and takes Bear's dagger with him. He sees Lady Furnival and her entourage.

Vocabulary
rushes (151)
kirtle (151)
pattens (151)
escapades (152)
slake (155)
furtively (156)
placating (158)
aggrieved (158)
privies (160)
buffeting (160)
disconcerted (161)
palfrey (162)
doffing (163)
personage (163)

Discussion Questions

1. How can you tell Widow Daventry is fond of Bear? (*They embrace and tease each other. They laugh together, and Crispin notices she seems to know more of Bear's business than he does. pp. 151–152*)

2. Who will inherit Lord Furnival's land and holdings? (*probably Lady Furnival since there are no legal heirs; Widow Daventry says that illegitimate sons may contest the lady's claim. pp. 154–155*)

3. What does the following statement mean: "a moment of silence in the midst of talk means Death's Angel is close at hand" (p. 155)? (*Answers will vary, but guide the students to see the author may be using the statement to foreshadow something.*)

4. Why does Crispin sneak out of the tavern even after Bear told him not to leave the room? (*Answers will vary but should include the idea that Crispin is uncomfortable in the room and very curious about the city. pp. 158–159*)

5. Why is Crispin so enthralled with white bread, the many lanes in the city, and Lady Furnival's procession? Discuss the irony involved in Crispin watching Lady Furnival process through the streets. (*He has never seen or tried these things before. It is ironic that Crispin is able to see the woman who has ordered his death to protect her power. pp. 160–163*)

6. **Prediction:** Will Crispin see Lady Furnival again?

Supplementary Activities

1. Social Studies: Have students research and find pictures of the dress of peasants in the Middle Ages. They should specifically find or prepare drawings or models of kirtles and wooden pattens, as worn by Widow Daventry (p. 151), and of the type of clothes and livery worn by Lady Furnival (p. 162). Students should discuss the differences in the attire worn by wealthy and poor members of a medieval community.

2. Writing: Have students write a journal entry regarding the following prompt: What does Bear mean symbolically when he says, "I'm a fool because I should like to be in Heaven before I die" (p. 158)?

3. Social Studies: Have students research funeral and mourning practices of the time period and compare and contrast the practices for serfs, like Asta, versus a lord

Chapters 38–41, pp. 164–185

Crispin wanders around the city and into the cathedral. Aycliffe sees him and yells for the soldiers to catch him. Crispin runs and is cornered by two men, but escapes. Bear finds him, scolds him, and returns him to Widow Daventry's inn. Crispin slips downstairs and eavesdrops on Bear talking to John Ball, a priest, about peasants rebelling over low wages and tyranny.

Vocabulary
tracery (165)
vestibule (167)
pelting (169)
nimbly (170)
ebb (173)
resumption (173)
serpentine (174)
laggards(175)
fervor (177)
vulnerable (184)

Discussion Questions

1. Why is Crispin intrigued with the cathedral? (*He has never seen a building so tall, and he is fascinated with the towers, arches, statues, stained glass, and burning candles. pp. 164–167*)

2. Why is Aycliffe in the cathedral? (*Answers will vary. Suggestions— He is looking for Crispin, mourning the death of Lord Fumival, or praying that his position is saved even though his lord has died. pp. 168–169*)

3. What does Crispin decide to do after he escapes from the soldiers and men? (*He decides to leave the town by following the walls around to the gate. pp. 171–172*)

4. How does Bear react when he finds Crispin? Why does Bear react this way? (*shouts, gets angry, embraces Crispin, and shows relief at finding him safe; Answers will vary, but students should discuss why Bear seems to care so much for Crispin and whether or not his emotions are genuine or if he has ulterior motives for protecting him. pp. 177–178*)

5. Why does Crispin sneak out of his room at the inn a second time? (*He is curious about John Ball and if John Ball might be part of the puzzle to his own identity. pp. 181–182*)

6. What does John Ball want to do? (*He wants to lead the peasants in a revolt to get better wages, decrease taxes, and put an end to the guilds. p. 183*)

7. What does Crispin conclude about Bear after eavesdropping on his conversation with John Ball? (*He thinks Bear is engaged in a rebellion and is a spy. p. 184*)

8. **Prediction:** Who do you think Crispin sees from the window in his room standing in the shadow of an overhanging building?

Supplementary Activities

1. Architecture: Have students research the architecture of the cathedrals in the Middle Ages and find drawings of arches, tracery, vestibules, statues, and stained glass, as described on pages 164–167 of the novel.

2. Writing: Have students write a journal entry about a time they were lost and couldn't find their way home or back to their parents. Have them describe the situation, their feelings, and their parents' reactions.

3. Social Studies: Have students research John Ball and the revolt he led later in 1381. They should write a short essay comparing and contrasting the true historical figure of John Ball to the character in *Crispin: The Cross of Lead*.

Chapters 42–48, pp. 185–214

The Feast of John the Baptist is celebrated in Great Wexly and many people visit the tavern, including the one-eyed youth from Lodgecot. Widow Daventry puts Crispin to work in the kitchen to hide him. Bear leaves, and Crispin sees the one-eyed youth pointing out Bear to Lord Furnival's men. Crispin follows Bear to warn him. The soldiers come to arrest them, but Crispin's shouts allow all but Bear to escape. Bear is taken by the soldiers to Furnival's palace. Crispin returns to the inn and hides in the secret room while soldiers search and tear up the tavern looking for him. Widow Daventry says they want Crispin dead, not Bear.

Vocabulary
peal (185)
leeks (190)
caterwauling (194)
broadswords (201)
chain mail (202)
protruded (207)

Discussion Questions

1. Who is the one-eyed youth trying to find? (*Answers will be either Bear, Crispin, and/or John Ball, but students should support their choices with good reasons. pp. 187–188*)

2. What does Widow Daventry tell Crispin about having Bear as a master? To what trouble is she referring? (*She says Bear is a good man and is good to Crispin. She warns Crispin not to let Bear mingle with troublemakers or things could get worse for both of them. Answers will vary. p. 192*)

3. What does Bear mean when he says, "less said, less to deny" (p. 194)? (*Answers will vary but should include the idea that the more you say, the more you are accountable for.*)

4. Why does Crispin say, "You've been protecting me...maybe I should be protecting you" (p. 195)? What does this say about how his character has changed? (*Crispin thinks Bear is a spy and getting ready to start a rebellion. He thinks the one-eyed youth is looking for Bear, and Widow Daventry told him earlier to keep Bear out of trouble. Answers will vary. pp. 192–195*)

5. In what "dangerous business" is Bear involved? (*He is in a group talking about a movement for freeing serfs, lowering rent on the lands, abolishing unfair taxes, and ending corruption in the government and the church. pp. 200–201*)

6. Re-read the speech Crispin overhears John Ball give (pp. 200–201). Analyze each sentence for its meaning and discuss. Interpret the speech based on what you have learned about the peasants and serfs of the time and their treatment by the lords of the lands. Discuss whether or not you agree with John Ball's ideas. (*Answers will vary.*)

7. What does John Ball mean when he says, "We are betrayed" (p. 203)? (*Answers will vary, but should include the idea that a person they thought was part of their group has told the soldiers about the meeting place.*)

8. What would have happened if Crispin had not gone to warn Bear and the other men? (*Answers will vary but should include the idea the men may have been arrested for speaking against the laws, parliaments, councilors, and church. They also may have been killed for treason. pp. 200–205*)

9. What does Widow Daventry think will happen to Bear now that he is captured? (*She feels he will be tortured until he tells Aycliffe where Crispin is and/or be killed. pp. 212–213*)

10. **Prediction:** Will Bear be tortured to such a degree that he will help Aycliffe find Crispin?

Supplementary Activities

1. Literary Analysis/Foreshadowing: Have students add to their foreshadowing list Crispin's sensation "that something dangerous was drawing in upon to us" (p. 188) and Widow Daventry's warning (p. 192).

2. Social Studies: Have students research the foods served at holidays/celebrations such as the Feast of St. John the Baptist as mentioned on pages 187 and 190 of the novel.

3. Drama: Ask each student to practice giving John Ball's speech (pp. 200–201) with feeling and emotion. Ask for a few volunteers to deliver the speech to the class.

Chapters 49–55, pp. 214–239

Widow Daventry reveals to Crispin that his cross reveals he is Furnival's son. Crispin learns more about his mother, father, grandfather, and why Lady Furnival and Aycliffe want him killed. The widow arranges for a man to sneak Crispin out of the city late at night, but Crispin goes to the White Stag tavern instead to seek help from John Ball and the rest of the brotherhood to free Bear. They refuse, but one leads Crispin to the palace where Crispin sneaks onto the second level and confronts Aycliffe.

Vocabulary

warrant (218)
fragmentary (221)
scabrous (225)
warren (227)
cowls (228)
succumb (229)
breach (233)
sconces (236)
spellbound (238)

Discussion Questions

1. What does Crispin discover about himself when Widow Daventry reveals what is written on the cross of lead? (*He learns he is the illegitimate son of Lord Furnival and that his mother is probably the daughter of Lord Douglas. When his mother was pregnant, she was banished to Stromford Village and not allowed to leave. She was protected by Lord Furnival. pp. 215–218*)

2. Why does Lady Furnival want a 13-year-old boy to be killed? (*Since Lord Furnival was Crispin's father, she is afraid Crispin, even though he is illegitimate, might try to make a claim on the land and palace she wants to keep. She does not want Crispin to take away her power. p. 217*)

3. What does Crispin figure out about the meeting in the forest he saw between Aycliffe and du Brey in Chapter 2? (*Richard du Brey was sent with a document to announce the impending death of Lord Furnival and the loss of protection for Asta and her son. Lady Furnival ordered Aycliffe to kill Asta's son so he would not make a claim as an heir. pp. 219–220*)

4. What does Crispin realize about bondage and freedom? (*He recalls John Ball's words—that no man shall enslave another, but each should stand free and equal. He realizes that he has lived in a type of bondage to the lord like many other peasants. He vows to free Bear since Bear helped him find his own freedom. pp. 222–223*)

5. Why does Crispin go to the White Stag tavern? What response does he receive there? (*He hopes to recruit John Ball and the other men of the brotherhood to help him free Bear. They offer no help. They say Bear will be tortured and may reveal their names to Aycliffe. They feel Bear is not in full support of their rebellion and that Crispin might turn them in. pp. 226–231*)

6. How does Crispin sneak into the palace? (*One member of the brotherhood shows him how to enter the palace. Crispin squeezes between the palace wall and an adjoining building, inches his way up to the second level, climbs over a statue, swings onto the balcony, and creeps inside. pp. 233–235*)

7. Why is Crispin spellbound in the palace? (*He has never seen so much gold and so many jewels. The walls and ceiling are covered with holy images. He sees an image of a knight kneeling before the Virgin Mary, and he realizes it must be a picture of Lord Furnival, his father. pp. 236-239*)

8. **Prediction:** Will Crispin become the next Lord Furnival?

Supplementary Activities

1. Literary Analysis: **Theme Development**—Have students summarize what Crispin finally realizes about freedom and bondage, as discussed on page 222 of the novel.

2. Latin: Have students research the meaning of the chant in Latin on page 232 of the novel.

3. Writing: Have students respond in their journals to the following prompt: What does Crispin mean when he says, "Just to see him in his exalted state, made me know with finality that I was not him. No, not any part. I was myself. What I had become" (p. 239)?

Chapters 56–58, pp. 240–262

Crispin argues with John Aycliffe and shows him the cross of lead that reveals he is the son of Lord Furnival. He accuses Aycliffe of killing Father Quinel. He bargains with Aycliffe to exchange the lead cross and any claim on being an heir for the release of Bear. At first, Aycliffe refuses—until Crispin puts a dagger to his throat. Bear is found badly battered in a cellar but is released. At the gates of the city Aycliffe breaks his promise, and a fight and scuffle ensue. Aycliffe dies, and Crispin and Bear leave the city as free men.

Vocabulary
disdain (240)
quaver (241)
summoning (244)
vaulted (247)
fore (247)
soot-blackened (248)
skittered (259)
impaled (260)
dub (261)
cantered (262)
unfettered (262)

Discussion Questions

1. What does Crispin say that shocks John Aycliffe? (*He says he is Crispin, Lord Furnival's son, and that he can prove it by what is written on his cross of lead. pp. 240–241*)

2. What do Aycliffe and Lady Furnival fear if Crispin lives? (*They fear he could become their lord. p. 242*)

3. Why does Crispin pull the dagger on Aycliffe and draw blood from Aycliffe's neck? (*Crispin is desperate to save Bear, and Aycliffe is not threatened by Crispin until Crispin attacks him. p. 244*)

4. What have Aycliffe's men done to Bear? (*He has been tortured. He is stretched upright on a ladder–like structure, arms bound over his head, and feet bound tightly. His body is almost naked, bloodstained with welts and whip marks. His hands are cut, his face bruised with an eye swollen shut, and his lips cut. pp. 249–250*)

5. Why does Bear ask Crispin, "did I betray you" (p. 250)? (*Bear has been so tortured he does not remember what he may or may not have told his oppressors. When he sees Crispin in the cell, he thinks Crispin is a prisoner, too. He is afraid he succumbed to the torture and told of Crispin's whereabouts.*)

6. Why does Crispin say he won't give Aycliffe the lead cross until they are beyond the city walls? (*Answers will vary but should include the idea that Crispin does not trust Aycliffe based on Aycliffe's past actions. p. 253*)

7. What does Bear call Aycliffe as they move toward the city gates? (*coward, traitor, oath breaker, murderer, and son of Lucifer. pp. 256–257*)

8. What happens to Aycliffe? (*He swings around to fight Crispin but Bear grabs him, pinning his arms to his sides, squeezing tighter and tighter until Aycliffe drops his sword. Bear raises Aycliffe over his head and throws him toward the soldiers where Aycliffe is impaled on their swords. pp. 259–260*)

9. What does Bear do for Crispin as they leave Great Wexly? (*He puts his two-pointed hat on Crispin's head and dubs him "Crispin of Stromford, a full member of the guild of free men." p. 261*)

10. Discuss the last paragraph of the book and how it relates to the themes of freedom, self-discovery, and self-reliance. (*Answers will vary. p. 262*)

11. **Prediction:** Will Crispin and Bear be hunted again?

Supplementary Activities

1. Literary Analysis: **Oxymoron**—Have students locate the oxymoron about a living deah (p. 242). As a class, discuss its meaning and why it is or is not significant to the story.

2. Social Studies: Have students research the types of torture used on prisoners in the latter part of the Middle Ages.

3. Drama: Group students in pairs and have them act out the scene on page 261 of the novel in which Bear dubs Crispin a full member of the guild of free men.

Post-reading Discussion Questions

1. Why didn't Crispin choose to make a claim as Lord Furnival's son after Aycliffe was killed?

2. If you could use only three adjectives to describe Crispin, what would they be?

3. What do you think Crispin's life will be like when he is 25 years old?

4. What important lessons does Crispin learn after his mother passes away?

5. How would the story be different if Asta, Crispin's mother, had not died?

6. What character, excluding Crispin and Bear, did you find most appealing? Why?

7. Can one be wealthy and free? Explain.

8. What did you learn about the Middle Ages from reading this book? What else would you like to know about this period in European history? Where could you go to find the information?

9. What are some of the strengths and limitations of first-person narrative? Give examples from the book to support your response.

10. How would the story be different if John Aycliffe were the narrator?

11. How would you compare the mood tone of pages 4–5 in Chapter One to the mood on pages 261–262 in the last chapter?

12. What have you learned about self-reliance from this book?

13. In what ways has this book affected your perception of "freedom"? Explain your response.

14. Would you recommend this book to a friend? Why or why not?

15. If you could interview Avi, the author of *Crispin: The Cross of Lead,* what three questions would you ask him?

16. Have you read a book similar to this one? What is it? How is it similar? How is it different?

17. Which did you enjoy most about the book—the setting, the characters, or the plot? Why?

18. How are Crispin's challenges and concerns like yours today? How are they different?

19. Discuss the following quote from the author, and how it relates to *Crispin: The Cross of Lead.* "Listen and watch the world around you. Try to understand why things happen. Don't be satisfied with answers others give you...work to get answers on your own. Understand why you believe things."

20. Avi says, "I believe reading is the key to writing. The more you read, the better your writing can be." What does he mean? Do you agree or disagree?

Post-reading Extension Activities

1. Create a symbol (no words) for Bear and one for Crispin that represents each of their qualities. You can draw the symbol, paint it, or design it on the computer.

2. Sort through the many words of wisdom given in the book. Choose one piece of advice that applies to your life and, in a brief essay, explain why it is valuable to you.

3. Try calligraphy using a special chiseled point pen. Look at the beginning of each chapter and the large capital letter with ornamental designs. Research "illumination" and find examples in books and/or on the Internet. If possible, use parchment paper to write a paragraph about the book in calligraphy.

4. The Christian canonical hours and bells mentioned in the book are: Matins or Lauds—sunrise morning prayers; Prime—6:00 a.m.–9:00 a.m.; Terce—9:00 a.m.–12 noon; Sext—12 noon–3:00 p.m.; None—3:00 p.m.–6:00 p.m.; Vespers—sunset evening prayers; Vigils—6:00 p.m.–6:00 a.m.; and Compline—last prayer of the day. Compare these times to the recommended hours of prayer to those in other religions, such as Judaism and Islam.

5. Find out more about the author. Write a letter to him regarding his books. Send to: Avi, c/o Dorothy Markinko, Agent, McIntosh & Otis, Inc., 475 Fifth Ave., New York, NY 10017.

6. View videos about the Middle Ages and use index cards to record new information you discover. Put the cards on a metal ring for quick reference.

7. Read another book by Avi and write a report comparing it to *Crispin: The Cross of Lead*.

8. Construct a scale model of a medieval village and surrounding lands or a peasant's hut.

9. Research the weapons mentioned in the novel: glaives, daggers, pikes, axes, bollocks, crossbows, and arrows. Search for pictures in books, dictionaries, and on the Internet.

10. Research the foods and herbs mentioned in the novel: barley bread, watered ale, cooked dried peas, apples, venison, rabbit, porridge, sweetmeats, lavender, parsley, sage, rosemary, onions, leeks, turnips, cabbages, and meat pies. Bring in samples of some of the foods for display.

11. Investigate music and songs of the Middle Ages. Borrow a recorder from the music teacher. Compose a tune for the song Bear sings on pages 109 and 261–262 of the novel.

12. Suppose the book is made into a film. Recommend who should play the role of Bear, Crispin, Aycliffe, and other characters.

13. Research the saints mentioned in the book. Write one sentence about each telling when they were canonized.

14. Draw and complete Venn diagrams on manor vs. hut and village vs. town using information from the book and other sources.

15. Create an acrostic for Crispin's name (Asta's son) at the beginning of the story. Write a second acrostic describing his name at the end of the story.

16. Write a letter that Bear might write to a friend describing Crispin and his feelings toward him. Use the type of words and language Bear would have used in medieval times.

17. Write dialogue of a conversation between Bear and Crispin that takes place after the book ends. Perform it with a partner for your classmates.

18. Plan a celebration for Midsummer's Day or Eve as mentioned in the book. Conduct research to gather more ideas on clothing (tunics, etc.), foods (destiny cakes, St. John's bread, etc.) activities (dances such as "Threading the Needle"), and entertainment (mummers, acrobats, musicians, etc.). Have the celebration in class. Be as authentic to the medieval times as possible.

Assessment for *Crispin: The Cross of Lead*

Assessment is an ongoing process. The following nine items can be completed during the novel study. Once finished, the student and teacher will check the work. Points may be added to indicate the level of understanding.

Name _____ Date _____

Student   **Teacher**

_____   _____   1. Draw a layout or sketch of Stromford Village based on the description in Chapters 1–4.

_____   _____   2. Illustrate and annotate three scenes from the book—one from the beginning, the middle, and the end.

_____   _____   3. Make a time line of the main events in the book with short annotations and illustrations.

_____   _____   4. Write an article for a magazine entitled "Before and After" to describe how Crispin changed throughout the book.

_____   _____   5. Complete your Story Map (page 8 of this guide).

_____   _____   6. Write a report explaining how the Crusades and the Plague led to the downfall of the feudal system in the 1400s.

_____   _____   7. Write a report on John Ball, his background, views and principles, and the Peasants' Revolt he led in 1381.

_____   _____   8. Select two of the following Old English laws mentioned in the book. Research them and write a one-page report on each to explain them: a. Wolf's head (p. 31); b. Claiming the right of sanctuary (p. 28); c. Gaining freedom after one year and a day (p. 32); d. Serf's rights and responsibilities, ancient freedoms (p. 25); e. Claim of runaway by first free man (p. 68).

_____   _____   9. Select a character from the novel and complete the chart on page 10 of this guide.

Glossary

The target vocabulary words are listed below by chapters and page numbers with the definition and part of speech as they are used in the novel.

Chapter 1, pp. 1–5
1. shroud (1): *n.* cloth used to wrap a body for burial
2. pauper (2): *n.* one who is very poor
3. steward (2): *n.* a person who is in charge of property finances or other affairs
4. astride (2): *adv.* with a leg on each side
5. deigned (3): *v.* to condescend
6. transgression (3): *n.* violation of a law or command
7. poaching (3): *v.* trespassing to take game or fish
8. forfeit (3): *v.* surrender, give up
9. manor (4): *n.* a lord's residence in a landed estate
10. tunic (4): *n.* loose fitting garment that goes to the knee
11. bracken (5): *n.* a fern with tough stems

Chapter 2, pp. 5–10
1. loying (5): *adj.* supplying too much of something, like sweetness or richness
2. welt (6): *n.* a bump raised on the skin from a blow or hit
3. murk (6): *n.* darkness
4. minions (6): *n.* subordinates
5. parchment (7): *n.* animal skin prepared for writing
6. affixed (7): *v.* to be attached, secured
7. transfixed (8): *v.* rendered motionless
8. avail (8): *n.* benefit, advantage
9. engulfed (10): *v.* to be overwhelmed by

Chapter 3, pp. 10–13
1. jibes (11): *n.* mocking, heckling remarks
2. embedded (11): *v.* to be fixed firmly, to be an integral part of
3. villeins (12): *n.* class of feudal serfs who were legally free, but bound to the land and their lord
4. serfs (12): *n.* persons bound to the land owned by a lord, lowest feudal class
5. ercenary (12): *adj.* motivated solely by money or material gain
6. farthing (12): *n.* coin worth one-fourth of a penny, also called a quarterpenny

Chapter 4, pp. 13–19
1. tolling (13): *adj.* sounding of a large bell at intervals
2. untoward (14): *adj.* unfavorable
3. cottar (14): *n.* one who holds little or no land of his/her own
4. reeve (15): *n.* high officer of local administration
5. wattle (15): *n.* poles intertwined with twigs or branches and used in construction
6. ford (17): *n.* a shallow place in a body of water
7. trestle (17): *adj.* with a horizontal beam supported by two pairs of slanted beams
8. run (18): *n.* a channel through which something flows
9. daub (18): *n.* plaster made with mud
10. commons (18): *n.* a piece of land belonging to and used by a community as a whole
11. fallow (18): *adj.* inactive field, plowed but unseeded
12. crofts (19): *n.* small enclosed fields or pastures near a house

Chapters 5–7, pp. 20–26

1. sowing (20): *v.* scattering seeds over the ground to grow
2. pealing (20): *v.* sounding or striking loudly
3. canonical (20): *adj.* pertaining to church laws
4. glaives (22): *n.* long poles with sharp blades attached
5. hue and cry (22): *n.* a loud cry formerly used to announce the pursuit of a felon
6. archer (23): *n.* one who shoots a bow and arrow
7. leagues (24): *n.* measures of distances of approximately 3 miles
8. moot (25): *n.* a meeting of the free men of an area

Chapter 8, pp. 27–36

1. alb (27): *n.* long white robe with tapered sleeves worn by a priest
2. wizened (27): *v.* shriveled, dried up
3. tonsured (27): *adj.* having a shaved crown
4. tallow (28): *n.* fats from animals or plants used to make candles
5. lime (28): *n.* calcium oxide combined with water and used as whitewash
6. font (28): *n.* a basin holding holy water in a church
7. genuflected (29): *v.* the act of bending the knee for worship
8. wolf's head (31): *n.* an outlaw designated so dangerous, anyone can kill the person

Chapters 9–13, pp. 37–54

1. crone (39): *n.* withered, witchlike older woman
2. foreboding (40): *n.* a dark sense of impending evil
3. rasping (40): *adj.* uttering in a grated voice
4. shillings (41): *n.* English coins worth 12 old pence, 20 shillings equals one British pound
5. disquiet (42): *n.* anxiety
6. proper (43): *n.* the main part
7. millrace (46): *n.* fast moving stream of water that drives a mill wheel
8. tumult (46): *n.* noise and commotion of a great crowd
9. albeit (48): *conj.* even though
10. rod (49): *n.* a measurement of 5.5 yards
11. lanced (50): *v.* pierced
12. dire (52): *adj.* so extreme as to require quick action or treatment

Chapters 14–15, pp. 54–60

1. lurching (55): *v.* rolling suddenly
2. distended (55): *adj.* stretched out in all directions
3. pillaged (56): *v.* stole goods by force
4. dell (57): *n.* small, secluded, wooded valley
5. hamlet (57): *n.* small village
6. trepidation (58): *n.* a state of dread or alarm
7. pestilence (59): *n.* a usually fatal epidemic
8. blight (59): *n.* disease resulting in death

Chapter 16, pp. 60–66

1. ruddy (61): *adj.* healthy, rosy color
2. bollock (62): *n.* type of dagger having a ball at the top and bottom of the handle
3. rents (64): *n.* holes or slits caused by ripping
4. cur (64): *n.* a mongrel dog
5. doddering (64): *adj.* senile, feeble-minded
6. parliaments (65): *n.* legislative bodies having power within states
7. venison (65): *n.* meat from a deer and other game
8. sweetmeats (65): *n.* candy, sweet delicacies

9. prudence (65): *n.* state of being cautious
10. belied (66): *v.* to be misrepresented, contradicted

Chapters 17–19, pp. 66–80
1. mockingly (67): *adv.* in an insincere manner
2. putrid (69): *adj.* rotten
3. screed (70): *n.* long, written or spoken tirade
4. pate (74): *n.* the head, especially the top
5. surname (76): *n.* a person's family name
6. henceforward (77): *adv.* from now on
7. wend (77): *v.* to proceed on or along
8. revels (77): *n.* noisy festivities
9. guildhalls (77): *n.* meeting places of business associations

Chapters 20–23, pp. 80–95
1. punctilious (83): *adj.* being conscientious
2. willy–nilly (83): *adv.* being willing and unwilling, haphazard, without choice
3. acolyte (83): *n.* an assistant at a church service
4. mummers (84): *n.* one who mimes; masked merrymakers
5. beguiled (84): *v.* amused, charmed
6. faltered (85): *v.* hesitated, halted
7. jeopardy (89): *n.* risk of loss, injury
8. stoke (90): *v.* to tend and fuel
9. agape (90): *adv.* wide, open
10. abated (90): *v.* to decrease, lessen

Chapters 24–27, pp. 95–114
1. mirth (97): *n.* merriment, easy laughter
2. livery (97): *n.* dress or insignia worn by members of a court of a feudal lord
3. heretic (100): *n.* a person who has controversial opinions and publicly disagrees with authority
4. sham (106): *n.* something false that is reported to be genuine
5. aloft (109): *adv.* high or higher up
6. spinney (111): *n.* a small grove
7. summit (111): *n.* the top of a mountain or hill
8. bade (112): *v.* issued a command
9. emblazoned (112): *v.* to be ornamented richly with color
10. paled (113): *v.* decreased in relative importance

Chapters 28–32, pp. 114–138
1. subdued (118): *v.* to be quieted, toned down
2. mollify (120): *v.* to soften, decrease temper
3. wry (122): *adj.* humorous with a touch of irony
4. snuffling (124): *v.* examining by smelling
5. penance (125): *n.* a sacrament in a church that includes confession and acceptance of punishment
6. beseech (125): *v.* to beg earnestly
7. mazer (126): *n.* large drinking bowl made of wood
8. gambols (127): *n.* playfully skipping, antics
9. dexterity (127): *n.* skill in use of the hands
10. malevolence (128): *n.* malice, ill will
11. lest (129): *conj.* for fear that
12. courier (130): *n.* a messenger on official business
13. enraptured (133): *v.* to be filled with delight
14. apprentice (138): *n.* one who works for and trains under another bound by an agreement

Chapters 33–34, pp. 139–150
1. pilgrim (139): *n.* religious devotee who travels to a shrine or sacred place
2. tinkers (141): *n.* traveling menders of metal utensils
3. press (143): *n.* a gathering in large numbers, pushing forward
4. portcullis (144): *n.* a sliding grill of iron or wood fixed in a gateway so it can be quickly lowered
5. gauntlet (145): *n.* two lines of people facing each other and holding weapons with which to hit person forced to run between them
6. timorous (145): *adj.* full of apprehension
7. palpable (146): *adj.* easily perceived
8. din (146): *n.* combination of loud and disagreeable noises
9. portentous (147): *adj.* full of amazement and wonder
10. cacophony (147): *n.* unharmonious sounds
11. swill (147): *n.* garbage, scraps fed to animals
12. solars (149): *n.* parlors or chambers exposed to the sun usually facing south

Chapters 35–37, pp. 150–163
1. rushes (151): *n.* grass-like marsh plants
2. kirtle (151): *n.* a knee-length tunic or long dress
3. pattens (151): *n.* wooden sandals or shoes
4. escapades (152): *n.* adventurous actions that often violate conventional standards
5. slake (155): *v.* to quench
6. furtively (156): *adv.* on the sly
7. placating (158): *v.* appeasing, granting concessions
8. aggrieved (158): *adj.* feeling distressed, feeling wrongly offended
9. privies (160): *n.* outhouses, outdoor bathrooms
10. buffeting (160): *v.* forcing against
11. disconcerted (161): *v.* to be frustrated and put into disorder
12. palfrey (162): *n.* a woman's saddled horse
13. doffing (163): *v.* tipping or removing
14. personage (163): *n.* a man or woman of distinction

Chapters 38–41, pp. 164–185
1. tracery (165): *n.* ornamental work with interlaced and branching lines
2. vestibule (167): *n.* small entranceway
3. pelting (169): *v.* moving at a vigorous pace
4. nimbly (170): *adv.* quickly with lightness
5. ebb (173): *v.* to fall away or decline
6. resumption (173): *n.* the act of beginning or taking up again
7. serpentine (174): *adj.* of or resembling the movement of a snake
8. laggards (175): *n.* stragglers
9. fervor (177): *n.* intense emotion
10. vulnerable (184): *adj.* susceptible to attack

Chapters 42–48, pp. 185–214
1. peal (185): *n.* loud burst of noise
2. leeks (190): *n.* plants similar to onions used in cooking
3. caterwauling (194): *v.* making discordant sounds or noises
4. broadswords (201): *n.* wide-blade cutting swords
5. chain mail (202): *n.* flexible armor made from metal links or scales
6. protruded (207): *v.* to be thrust outward

Chapters 49–55, pp. 214–239

1. warrant (218): *n.* justification for action
2. fragmentary (221): *adj.* consisting of broken parts
3. scabrous (225): *adj.* rough, off color
4. warren (227): *n.* an overcrowded place of habitation
5. cowls (228): *n.* the hoods of robes worn by monks
6. succumb (229): *v.* give up, give in
7. breach (233): *n.* a gap
8. sconces (236): *n.* decorative wall brackets
9. spellbound (238): *adj.* entranced

Chapters 56–58, pp. 240–262

1. disdain (240): *n.* an attitude of contempt, scorn
2. quaver (241): *n.* tremble
3. summoning (244): *v.* calling forth
4. vaulted (247): *adj.* arched
5. fore (247): *n.* front part
6. soot-blackened (248): *adj.* covered with particles produced by the incomplete combustion of wood
7. skittered (259): *v.* moved rapidly
8. impaled (260): *v.* pierced with a sharp stake or point
9. dub (261): *v.* to honor with a title or description
10. cantered (262): *v.* to ride slower than a gallop but faster than a trot
11. unfettered (262): *v.* liberated, freed